TO

....

FROM

....

NOTE FROM THE AUTHOR

I often have the impression that the words I write have more lasting value than my life, and I sense that the higher I reach in my writing about the spiritual life, the more I misrepresent my own disorderly life. It is far easier, I find, to edit words than to edit life.

I can only write with passion about my own experience, not yours. Yet somehow my rendering of church, family, and halting steps toward faith may provoke a response in the reader, like the harmonic overtones from a plucked guitar string.

Writing has afforded me a way to work out my faith, word by word. And to my astonishment my words have helped encourage others in their faith. With this journal, my hope is that you will find the words to write with passion about your life, your faith, your journey of grace.

The selections included are from work written over several decades, appearing in various books and articles. As you read through them, I pray that you will be inspired to write your own notes and that they will be infused with grace.

Philip Yancey

Philip Yancey serves as editor-at-large for *Christianity Today* magazine. He has written twelve Gold Medallion Award–winning books and won two ECPA Book of the Year awards for *What's So Amazing About Grace?* and *The Jesus I Never Knew.* Four of his books have sold over one million copies. He lives with his wife in Colorado.

GRACE NOTES

PHILIP YANCEY

...inspired by life

THE LAST BEST WORD

*A*s a writer I've found that words tend to spoil over the years, like old meat. Their meaning rots away.

Consider the word *charity*, for instance. When King James translators contemplated the highest form of love they settled on the word *charity* to convey it. Nowadays we hear the scornful protest, "I don't want your charity!"

Perhaps I keep circling back to *grace* because it is one grand theological word that has not spoiled. I call it "the last best word" because every English usage I can find retains some of the glory of the original. Like a vast aquifer, the word underlies our proud civilization, reminding us that good things come not from our own efforts, rather by the grace of God.

Grace is indeed amazing. It contains the essence of the gospel, as a drop of water can contain the image of the sun. The world thirsts for grace in ways it does not even recognize; little wonder the hymn "Amazing Grace" edged its way onto the Top Ten charts two hundred years after composition. For a society that seems adrift, without moorings, I know of no better place to drop an anchor of faith.

WHAT'S SO AMAZING ABOUT GRACE?, 12–13

But where sin increased, grace increased all the more.

ROMANS 5:20

GOD CAME CLOSE

What difference did Jesus make? Both for God and for us, he made possible an *intimacy* that had never before existed. In the Old Testament, Israelites who touched the sacred Ark of the Covenant fell down dead; but people who touched Jesus, the Son of God in flesh, came away healed. To Jews who would not pronounce or even spell out the letters in God's name, Jesus taught a new way of addressing God: *Abba*, or "Daddy." In Jesus, God came close.

The book of Hebrews explores this startling new advance in intimacy. We can now "approach the throne of grace with confidence," without fear. Charging boldly into the Most Holy Place—no image could hold more shock value for Jewish readers. Yet at the moment of Jesus' death, a thick curtain inside the temple literally ripped in two from top to bottom, breaking open the Most Holy Place. Therefore, concludes Hebrews, "Let us draw near to God."

Jesus contributes at least this to the problem of disappointment with God: because of him, we can come to God directly. We need no human mediator, for God's own self became one.

DISAPPOINTMENT WITH GOD, 124–25

The Word became flesh and made his dwelling among us.

JOHN 1:14

Prozac Jesus

ow would Jesus have scored on a personality profile test?

The personality that emerges from the Gospels differs radically from the image of Jesus I grew up with, an image I now recognize in some of the older Hollywood films about Jesus. In those films, Jesus recites his lines evenly and without emotion. He strides through life as the one calm character among a cast of flustered extras. Nothing rattles him. He is, in short, the Prozac Jesus.

In contrast, the Gospels present a man who has such charisma that people will sit three days straight, with empty stomachs, just to hear his riveting words. He seems excitable, impulsively "moved with compassion," or "filled with pity." Three times, at least, he cried in front of his disciples. He did not hide his fears or hesitate to ask for help.

Jesus quickly established intimacy with the people he met. Whether talking with a woman at a well, a religious leader in a garden, or a fisherman by a lake, he cut instantly to the heart of the matter, and soon these people revealed to Jesus their innermost secrets. Jesus drew out a hunger so deep that people crowded around him just to touch his clothes.

THE JESUS I NEVER KNEW, 88–89

When Jesus had finished saying these things, the crowds were amazed at his teaching, because he taught as one who had authority, and not as their teachers of the law.

MATTHEW 7:28–29

GETTING A LIFE

"The glory of God is a person fully alive," said the second-century theologian Irenaeus. Sadly, that description does not reflect the image many people have of modern Christians.

Author Frederick Buechner decided once to turn his literary skills to exploring the lives of saints. The first three he chose—Brendan, Godric, and the biblical Jacob—surprised him, for the more he researched them, the more skeletons in the closet he uncovered. What made this unsavory trio saintly? he asked himself. He finally settled on the word "life-giver." Passionate, risk-taking, courageous, each of the three made those around him feel more alive, not less.

When I heard Buechner give that definition of saintliness, I thought immediately of my friend Bob. I have never met anyone more fully alive. He took in stray animals, did carpentry chores for friends, climbed mountains, sky-dived, learned to cook, built his own house. Although Bob rarely used religious words, I noticed that everyone around him, including me, felt more alive after spending time with him. He radiated the kind of pleasure in the world of matter that God must feel. By Buechner's definition, at least, Bob was a saint.

"BACK PAGE" COLUMN, *CHRISTIANITY TODAY*
OCTOBER 23, 2000

I have been crucified with Christ and I no longer live,
but Christ lives in me.

GALATIANS 2:20

INVISIBLE IMPACT

In the Old Testament, faithful believers seemed shocked when suffering came their way. They expected God to reward their faithfulness with prosperity and comfort. But the New Testament shows a remarkable change. As Peter advised suffering Christians, "This suffering is all part of the work God has given you. Christ, who suffered for you, is your example. Follow in his steps" (1 Peter 2:21 TLB).

According to Paul, at the cross Christ triumphed over the cosmic powers—defeating them not with power but with self-giving love. The cross of Christ may have assured the final outcome, but battles remain for us to fight.

We will never know, in this life, the full significance of our actions here, for much takes place invisible to us. When a pastor in an oppressive country goes to prison for his peaceful protest, when a social worker moves into an urban ghetto, when a couple refuses to give up on a difficult marriage, when a parent waits with undying hope and forgiveness for the return of an estranged child—in all these sufferings, large and small, there is the assurance of a deeper level of meaning, of a sharing in Christ's own redemptive victory.

WHERE IS GOD WHEN IT HURTS?, 231–32

The Lord is close to the brokenhearted and saves those
who are crushed in spirit.

PSALM 34:18

CHILDREN AND LOVERS

*M*ore than any other word pictures, God chooses "children" and "lovers" to describe our mutual relationship.

The Old Testament abounds with husband-bride imagery. God woos people, and dotes on them like a lover doting on his beloved. When they fail to respond, God feels hurt, spurned, like a jilted lover. The New Testament often uses the same imagery, picturing the church as "the bride of Christ." Shifting metaphors, it also announces that we are God's children, with all the rights and privileges of worthy heirs. Jesus (the "only begotten" Son of God) came, we're told, to make possible our adoption as sons and daughters in God's family. God looks upon us as we might look upon our own child, or our lover.

As I read the Bible, it seems clear that God satisfies an eternal appetite by loving individual human beings. And perhaps, when the secrets of the universe are revealed, we will learn an underlying purpose of parenthood and romantic love. It may be that God has granted us these times of *specialness* to awaken us to the mere possibility of infinite love. Of that love, our most intimate experiences here on earth are mere glimpses.

I WAS JUST WONDERING, 163–66

Yet to all who received him, to those who believed in his name,
he gave the right to become children of God.

ALCOHOLIC TEACHERS

*A*lcoholics Anonymous meets needs in a way that the local church does not—or at least did not for my friend. I asked him to name the one quality missing in the local church that AA had somehow provided. He said softly this one word: dependency.

"None of us can make it on our own—isn't that why Jesus came?" he explained. "Yet most church people give off a self-satisfied air of piety or superiority. I don't sense them consciously leaning on God or on each other. Their lives appear to be in order. What I hate most about myself, my alcoholism, was the one thing God used to bring me back to him. Because of it, I know I can't survive without God. I have to depend on him to make it through each and every day. Maybe God is calling us alcoholics to teach the saints what it means to be dependent on him and on his community on earth."

From my friend's midnight church I learned the need for humility, total honesty, and radical dependence—on God and on a community of compassionate friends. As I thought about it, these qualities seemed exactly what Jesus had in mind when he founded his church.

CHURCH: WHY BOTHER?, 51–52

Remain in me, and I will remain in you. No branch can bear
fruit by itself; it must remain in the vine.
Neither can you bear fruit unless you remain in me.

JOHN 15:4

MONEY WORRIES

esus has more to say on money than almost any other topic. Yet two thousand years later Christians have trouble agreeing on exactly what he *does* say. One reason is that he rarely gives "practical" advice. He avoids comment on specific economic systems and, as in Luke 12, refuses to get involved in personal disputes about finances. Jesus sees money primarily as a *spiritual* force.

Money operates much like idolatry. It can catch hold and dominate a person's life, diverting attention away from God. Jesus challenges people to break free of money's power—even if it means giving it all away.

Luke 12 offers a good summary of Jesus' attitude toward money. He does not condemn all possessions. But he strongly warns against putting faith in money to secure the future.

Jesus urges his listeners to seek treasure in the kingdom of God, for such treasure can benefit them in this life and the next one too. "Do not worry," he says. Rather, trust God to provide your basic needs. Better to trust in the God who lavishes care on the whole earth than to spend your life worrying about money and possessions.

MEET THE BIBLE, 455–56

But seek first his kingdom and his righteousness, and all these things will be given to you as well. Therefore do not worry about tomorrow, for tomorrow will worry about itself.

MATTHEW 6:33

Tab. 36

DISTRESS SIGNALS

hy did Jesus have to suffer and die? Among the answers the Bible gives is this most mysterious answer: suffering served as a kind of "learning experience" for God. Such words seem faintly heretical, but I am merely following Hebrews: "Although he was a son, he learned obedience from what he suffered" (5:8).

These words surely mean at least this: the incarnation had meaning for God as well as for us. On one level, of course, God understood physical pain. But had a Spirit ever felt physical pain? Not until the incarnation.

In some incomprehensible way, because of Jesus, God hears our groans differently. "For we do not have a high priest who is unable to sympathize with our weaknesses, but we have one who has been tempted in every way, just as we are—yet was without sin" (4:14). We have a high priest who, having graduated from the school of suffering, "is able to deal gently with those who are ignorant and are going astray, since he himself is subject to weakness" (5:2).

We need no longer cry into the abyss, "Hey, are you listening?" By joining us on earth, Jesus gave visible, historical proof that God hears our groans, and even groans them with us.

"DISTRESS SIGNALS," CHRISTIANITY TODAY
OCTOBER 8, 1990

*In bringing many sons to glory, it was fitting that God,
for whom and through whom everything exists, should make the
author of their salvation perfect through suffering.*

HEBREWS 2:10

DENYING MYSELF

*W*hat are the implications of Jesus' statement that I need to lose my life for his sake? What does he mean, specifically, when he says I should deny that self I have come to know fairly well over the years, take up a cross, and follow him?

Self-denial first strikes at my basic identity. I am by nature a selfish creature, and I spend my time with a body and personality unique in all the world. It inevitably follows that I begin viewing the world through a viewpoint, making value judgments based on how things align with my perspective, and imposing my likes and dislikes on others around me.

In his essay, "The Trouble with X," C. S. Lewis points out that we spot a fatal flaw in almost everyone we meet, even our closest friends. Yet we almost never see that fatal flaw in ourselves.

Denying myself starts with a full and repentant acceptance of the fatal flaw within me. Regardless of my accomplishments, my sophistication, my admirable traits, I must come to the humbling ground where I acknowledge I am not different from, but like every person who has ever lived. I am a sinner.

*Do not think of yourself more highly than you ought,
but rather think of yourself with sober judgment, in accordance
with the measure of faith God has given you.*

ROMANS 12:3

Two Cheers for Guilt

"*L*ove means never having to say you're sorry," proclaimed a sappy romance novel from the 1970s. I have come to believe the opposite, that love means precisely having to say you're sorry. A sense of guilt, vastly underappreciated, deserves our gratitude, for only such a powerful force can nudge us toward repentance and reconciliation with those we have harmed.

Yet guilt represents danger as well. I have known Christians who go through life with a hyper-attention to defects, terrified that they are somehow offending one of God's laws. A mature Christian learns to discriminate between false guilt inherited from parents, church, or society and true guilt as a response to breaking God's laws clearly revealed in the Bible.

Just as the physical body speaks to us in the language of pain so that we will attend to the injury site, the soul speaks to us in the language of guilt so that we will take the steps necessary for healing. The goal in both is to restore health.

True saints do not get discouraged over their faults, for they recognize that a person who feels no guilt can never find healing.

"BACK PAGE" COLUMN, CHRISTIANITY TODAY
NOVEMBER 18, 2002

If we claim to be without sin, we deceive ourselves and the truth
is not in us. If we confess our sins, he is faithful and just and will
forgive us our sins and purify us from all unrighteousness.

1 JOHN 1:8–10

THREE TEARS

Three times that we know of, suffering drove Jesus to tears. He wept when his friend Lazarus died.

Another time, tears came to Jesus when he looked out over Jerusalem and realized the fate awaiting that fabled city. I sense in that spasm of emotional pain something akin to what a parent feels when a son or daughter goes astray.

Finally, Hebrews tells us, Jesus "offered up loud cries and tears to the one who could save him from death." But of course he was not saved from death. Is it too much to say that Jesus himself asked the question that haunts most of us at one time or another: Does God care?

Jesus faced pain much as I do. He experienced sorrow, fear, abandonment, and something approaching even desperation. Yet he endured because he knew that at the center of the universe lived his Father, a God of love he could trust regardless of how things appeared at the time.

Jesus' response to suffering people provides a glimpse into the heart of God. God is not the unmoved Absolute, but rather the Loving One who draws near.

THE JESUS I NEVER KNEW, 160–61

Because he himself suffered when he was tempted, he is able to help those who are being tempted.

HEBREWS 2:18

THE COMPANY HE KEPT

Jesus was the friend of sinners. They liked being around him and yearned for his company. Meanwhile, legalists found him shocking, even revolting. What was Jesus' secret that we have lost?

The Gospels mention eight occasions when Jesus accepted an invitation to dinner. Three of these were normal social occasions among friends. The other five, however, defy all rules of social propriety.

In Palestine, stern laws enforced the stigma against leprosy: the afflicted had to live outside city walls and yell, "Unclean!" when they approached anyone. Yet Jesus ignored those rules and reclined at the table of a man who wore that stigma as part of his name.

At least one other time Jesus accepted hospitality from a prominent Pharisee. Like double agents, the religious leaders were following him around and inviting him to meals while scrutinizing his every move. Provocatively, despite it being the Sabbath, Jesus healed a man from dropsy, and then he drew a stinging contrast between the social-climbing banquets of the Pharisees and God's banquet spread for "the poor, the crippled, the blind and the lame." The Gospels record no other meals with prominent citizens, and I can easily understand why: Jesus hardly made for a soothing dinner guest.

THE JESUS I NEVER KNEW, 149–50

She wet my feet with her tears and wiped them with her hair....
Therefore, I tell you, her many sins have been forgiven—for she
loved much. But he who has been forgiven little loves little.

LUKE 7:44, 47

HIDDEN GOD

Human longing for the actual presence of God may crop up almost anywhere. But we dare not make sweeping claims about the promise of God's intimate presence unless we take into account those times when God seems absent. At some point nearly everyone must face the fact of God's hiddenness.

For those who suffer, and those who stand beside them, Job offers up an important lesson. Doubts and complaints are valid responses, not symptoms of weak faith—so valid, in fact, that God made sure the Bible included them all. One does not expect to find the arguments of God's adversaries bound into the Bible, but nearly all of them make an appearance. The Bible seems to anticipate our disappointments, as if God grants us in advance the weapons in opposition, as if God too understands the cost of sustaining faith.

And, because of Jesus, perhaps God does understand. At Gethsemane and Calvary in some inexpressible way God himself was forced to confront the hiddenness of God. "God striving with God" is how Martin Luther summarized the cosmic struggle played out on two crossbeams of wood. On that dark night, God learned the full extent of what it means to feel God-forsaken.

DISAPPOINTMENT WITH GOD, 232–33

O my God, I cry out by day, but you do not answer, by night, and am not silent.

PSALM 22:2

UNTAMING JESUS

In writing a book about Jesus, one impression struck me more forcefully than any other: we have tamed him. The Jesus I learned about as a child was sweet and inoffensive, the kind of person whose lap you want to climb onto: someone like television's cuddly Mister Rogers, only with a beard. Indeed Jesus did have qualities of gentleness and compassion that attracted little children. Mister Rogers, however, he assuredly was not.

I realized this fact when I studied the Sermon on the Mount. "Blessed are the poor. Blessed are the persecuted. Blessed are those who mourn." These sayings have a soft, proverbial ring to them— unless you happen to know someone poor, persecuted, or mourning.

I came away from my study of Jesus both comforted and terrified. Jesus came to earth "full of grace and truth," said John: his truth comforts my intellectual doubts even as his grace comforts my emotional doubts. And yet I also encountered a terrifying aspect of Jesus, one that I had never learned about in Sunday school. Did anyone go away from Jesus' presence feeling satisfied about his or her life?

The Jesus I met in the Gospels was anything but tame.

"UNWRAPPING JESUS," CHRISTIANITY TODAY
JUNE 17, 1996

[Jesus] drove all from the temple area...and overturned their tables.
To those who sold doves he said, "Get these out of here!
How dare you turn my Father's house into a market!"

JOHN 2:15–16

GOD'S VOICES

Think of God's plan as a series of Voices. The first Voice, thunderingly loud, had certain advantages. When the Voice spoke from the trembling mountain at Sinai, no one could deny it. Yet, amazingly, even those who heard the Voice and feared it soon learned to ignore it.

The Voice modulated with Jesus, the *Word* made flesh. For a few decades the Voice of God took on the rural accent of a country Jew in Palestine. It was a normal human voice, and though it spoke with authority, it did not cause people to flee. Jesus' voice was soft enough to debate against, soft enough to kill.

After Jesus departed, the Voice took on new forms. On the day of Pentecost, tongues—*tongues*—of fire fell on the faithful, and the church, God's body, began to take shape. That last Voice is as close as breath, as gentle as a whisper. It is the most vulnerable Voice of all, and the easiest to ignore. The Bible says the Spirit can be "quenched" or "grieved." Yet the Spirit is also the most intimate Voice. In our moments of weakness, when we do not know what to pray, the Spirit within intercedes for us with groans that words cannot express.

DISAPPOINTMENT WITH GOD, 151–52

In the same way, the Spirit helps us in our weakness. We do not know what we ought to pray for, but the Spirit himself intercedes for us with groans that words cannot express.

ROMANS 8:26

Tab. 36

NO SHORTCUTS

believe most of the questions about guidance are misdirected. They are the typically impatient demands of us Americans who want a shortcut to the "magic," the benefit of relating to Almighty God. There is no shortcut, no magic, at least not that anyone can reduce to a three-point outline. There is only the possibility of a lifetime search for intimacy with a God who sometimes seems close and sometimes far, sometimes seems loving and sometimes forgetful.

Does God guide? Yes, I believe. Most times God guides in subtle ways, by feeding ideas into our minds, speaking through a nagging sensation of dissatisfaction, inspiring us to choose better than we otherwise would have done, bringing to the surface hidden dangers of temptation, and perhaps by rearranging certain circumstances. God's guidance will supply real help, but in ways that will not overwhelm my freedom.

True guidance cannot resemble magic, a way for God to give us shortcuts and genie bottles. It must, rather, occur in the context of a committed relationship between you and your God. Once that relationship exists, divine guidance becomes not an end in itself but merely one more means God uses in nourishing faith.

GUIDANCE BOOKLET, 15–16

Trifolium pallidum

Show me your ways, O Lord, teach me your paths.

PSALM 25:4

GOD'S FACE

Much of my career as a writer has revolved around the problem of pain. I hear from readers of my books, and their anguished stories give human faces to my doubts.

I remember a youth pastor in Colorado who had just learned his wife and baby daughter were dying of AIDS. "How can I talk to my youth group about a loving God?" he asked. Another was a blind man who had invited a recovering drug addict into his home as an act of mercy. He had just learned the recovering addict was carrying on an affair with his wife.

I have learned not even to attempt an answer to the why questions. One question, however, no longer gnaws at me as it once did: the question "Does God care?" I know of only one way to answer that question, and for me it has proved decisive: Jesus is the answer. In Jesus, God gave us a face. If you wonder how God feels about the suffering on this groaning planet, look at that face. By no means did Jesus solve the problem of pain but he did signify an answer to the question *Does God care?*

"DO I MATTER? DOES GOD CARE?"
CHRISTIANITY TODAY, NOVEMBER 22, 1993

*He was pierced for our transgressions, he was crushed for
our iniquities; the punishment that brought us
peace was upon him, and by his wounds we are healed.*

ISAIAH 53:5

HAPPY ENDING

In its "plot," the Bible ends up very much where it began. The broken relationship between God and human beings has healed over at last, and the curse of Genesis 3 is lifted. Borrowing images from Eden, Revelation pictures a river and a tree of life. But this time a great city replaces the garden setting—a city filled with worshipers of God. No death or sadness will ever darken that scene.

Revelation promises that our longings are not mere fantasies. They will come true. When we awake in the new heaven and new earth, we will have at last whatever we have longed for.

In the Bible, heaven is not an afterthought or optional belief. It is the final justification of all creation. The Bible never belittles human tragedy and disappointment but it does add one key word: *temporary*. What we feel now, we will not always feel.

For people who feel trapped in pain or in a broken home, in economic misery or in fear—for all those people, for all of us, heaven promises a future time, far longer and more substantial than the time we spend on earth, a time of health and wholeness and pleasure and peace.

MEET THE BIBLE, 684–85

God himself will be with them and be their God. He will wipe every tear from their eyes. There will be no more death or mourning or crying or pain, for the old order of things has passed away.

REVELATION 21:3-4

BODY PARTS

*H*ow can we sense God's love now that Jesus has ascended to the Father?

One New Testament answer centers around "the body of Christ." When Jesus left, he turned over his mission to flawed and bumbling men and women.

A careful reading of the four Gospels shows that this new arrangement was what Jesus had in mind all along. "I will build my church," he declared, "and the gates of hell shall not prevail against it" (Matthew 16:18 KJV).

Jesus' decision to operate as the invisible head of a large body with many members affects our view of suffering. It means that he often relies on us to help one another cope. The phrase "the body of Christ" expresses well what we are called to do: to represent in flesh what Christ is like. The apostle Paul must have had something like that process in mind when he wrote these words: "[God] comforts us in all our troubles, so that we can comfort those in any trouble with the comfort we ourselves have received from God. For just as the sufferings of Christ flow over into our lives, so also through Christ our comfort overflows" (2 Corinthians 1:4–5).

WHERE IS GOD WHEN IT HURTS?, 235–37

Now you are the body of Christ, and each one of you is a part of it.

1 CORINTHIANS 12:27

FAILSAFE

*A*s I reconsider my own assumptions about relating to God, I now see them as misguided and simplistic. From childhood I inherited an image of God as a stern teacher passing out grades.

Almost everything about that analogy, I have learned, contradicts the Bible and distorts the relationship. In the first place, God's approval depends not on my "good conduct" but on God's grace. I could never earn grades high enough to pass a teacher's perfect standards—and, thankfully, I do not have to. In addition, a relationship with God does not switch on or off depending on my behavior. God does not send me to a vacant room down the hall when I disobey.

Quite the opposite. The times when I feel most estranged from God can bring on a sense of desperation, which presents a new starting point for grace.

I tend to project onto God my understanding of how human relationships work, including the assumption that betrayal permanently destroys relationship. God, however, seems undeterred by betrayal. As [Martin] Luther remarked, we are always at the same time sinners, righteous, and penitent. The halting, stuttered expressions of love we offer may not measure up to what God wants, but like any parent, God accepts what the children offer.

REACHING FOR THE INVISIBLE GOD, 192–93

Where can I go from your Spirit? Where can I flee from your presence? If I go up to the heavens, you are there; if I make my bed in the depths, you are there.

PSALM 139:7-8

POWER SHARING

I used to feel spiritually inferior because I had not experienced the more spectacular manifestations of the Spirit and could not point to any bona fide "miracles" in my life. Increasingly, though, I have come to see that what I value may differ greatly from what God values. Jesus, often reluctant to perform miracles, considered it progress when he departed earth and entrusted the mission to his flawed disciples. Like a proud parent, God seems to take more delight as a spectator of the bumbling achievements of stripling children than in any self-display of omnipotence.

From God's perspective, if I may speculate, the great advance in human history may be what happened at Pentecost, which restored the direct correspondence of spirit to Spirit that had been lost in Eden. I want God to act in direct, impressive, irrefutable ways. God wants to "share power" with the likes of me, accomplishing his work through people, not despite them.

"Take me seriously! Treat me like an adult, not a child!" is the cry of every teenager. God honors that request, making me a partner for kingdom work, granting me freedom in full knowledge that I will abuse it.

REACHING FOR THE INVISIBLE GOD, 182–84

I no longer call you servants, because a servant does not know his master's business. Instead, I have called you friends, for everything that I learned from my Father I have made known to you.

JOHN 15:15–16

PAIN'S ALCHEMY

*C*hristianity contains within it paradoxes that would make little sense apart from Jesus' life and death. Consider one paradox: although poverty and suffering are "bad things," yet at the same time they can be called "blessed." This pattern of bad transmuted into good finds its fullest expression in Jesus. By taking it on himself, Jesus dignified pain, showing us how it can be transformed.

We feel pain as an outrage; Jesus did too, which is why he performed miracles of healing. In Gethsemane he did not pray, "Thank you for this opportunity to suffer," but rather pled desperately for an escape. And yet he was willing to undergo suffering in service of a higher goal.

In the ultimate alchemy of all history, God took the worst thing that could possibly happen—the appalling execution of the innocent Son—and turned it into the final victory over evil and death. It was an act of unprecedented cunning, turning the design of evil into the service of good, an act that holds within it a promise for all of us. The unimaginable suffering of the cross was fully redeemed: it is by his *wounds* that we are healed (Isaiah 53:5), by his weakness that we are made strong.

WHERE IS GOD WHEN IT HURTS?, 230-31

He fell with his face to the ground and prayed, "My Father, if it is possible, may this cup be taken from me."

MATTHEW 26:39

EXTREME MAKEOVER

*R*arely do I wake up in the morning full of faith. "Don't you know that you yourselves are God's temple and that God's Spirit lives in you?" Paul asked the Corinthians. If God himself lives inside me, shouldn't I wake up with that knowledge and live in constant awareness all day long? Alas, I do not. After an organ transplant, doctors must use antirejection drugs to suppress the immune system or else the body will throw off the newly grafted member. I have come to see the Holy Spirit as a power living inside me that keeps me from throwing off the new identity God has implanted. My spiritual immune system needs daily reminders that God's presence *belongs* within me and is no foreign object.

Absorbing a new identity requires an act of will. Rather than rushing from one task to the next, pause for a moment and recognize the time between times. Before dialing the phone, pause and think about the person on the other end. After reading from a book, pause and think back through how you were moved. After watching a television show, pause and ask what it contributed to your life. Before reading the Bible, pause and ask for a spirit of attention.

REACHING FOR THE INVISIBLE GOD, 167–69

And if the Spirit of him who raised Jesus from the dead is living in you, he who raised Christ from the dead will also give life to your mortal bodies through his Spirit, who lives in you.

ROMANS 8:11

ROSETTA STONE

*S*tep back for a moment and contemplate God's point of view. A spirit unbound by time and space, God had borrowed material objects now and then—a burning bush, a pillar of fire—to make an obvious point on planet Earth. In Jesus, something new happened: God *became* one of the planet's creatures.

Because of Jesus we need never question God's desire for intimacy. Does God really want close contact with us? Jesus gave up heaven for it. In person he reestablished the original link between God and human beings, between seen and unseen worlds.

H. Richard Niebuhr likened the revelation of God in Christ to the Rosetta stone. Before its discovery scholars could only guess at the meaning of Egyptian hieroglyphics. One unforgettable day they uncovered a dark stone that rendered the same text in three different languages. By comparing the translations side by side, they mastered hieroglyphics and could now see clearly into a world they had known only in a fog.

Niebuhr goes on to say that Jesus allows us to "reconstruct our faith." We can trust God because we trust Jesus. If we doubt God, or find him incomprehensible, unknowable, the very best cure is to gaze steadily at Jesus, the Rosetta stone of faith.

REACHING FOR THE INVISIBLE GOD, 135–39

Let us fix our eyes on Jesus, the author and perfecter of our faith.

HEBREWS 12:2

QUIET CARE

How do I help someone else in need? I have learned that simple availability is the most powerful force we can contribute to help calm the fears of others.

We rightly disparage Job's three friends for their insensitive response to his suffering. But read the account again: when they came, they sat in silence beside Job for seven days and seven nights before opening their mouths. As it turned out, those were the most eloquent moments they spent with him. Instinctively, I shrink back from people who are in pain. Who can know whether they want to talk about their predicament or not? Do they want to be consoled, or cheered up? What good can my presence possibly do? My mind spins out these rationalizations and as a result I end up doing the worst thing possible: I stay away.

No one offers the name of a philosopher when I ask the question, "Who helped you most?" Most often they answer by describing a quiet, unassuming person. Someone who was there whenever needed, who listened more than talked, who didn't keep glancing down at a watch, who hugged and touched, and cried. In short, someone who was available, and came on the sufferer's terms and not their own.

WHERE IS GOD WHEN IT HURTS?, 176–77

Praise be to the God and Father of our Lord Jesus Christ...who comforts us in all our troubles, so that we can comfort those in any trouble with the comfort we ourselves have received from God.

2 CORINTHIANS 1:3-4

Tab. 36

LACK OF ALTERNATIVES

feel kinship with those who find it impossible to believe or
find it impossible to keep on believing in the face of apparent betrayal.
I have been in a similar place at times, and I marvel that God bestowed
on me an unexpected gift of faith. Examining my own periods of
faithlessness, I see in them all manner of unbelief. Something, though,
keeps drawing me back to God. What? I ask myself.

"This is a hard teaching. Who can accept it?" said Jesus' disciples.
Jesus' listeners found themselves simultaneously attracted and repelled.
As his words sank in, one by one the crowd of onlookers and followers
slouched away, leaving only the twelve. "You do not want to leave too,
do you?" Jesus asked them. As usual, Simon Peter spoke up: "Lord, to
whom shall we go?"

That, for me, is the bottom-line answer to why I stick around.
To my shame, I admit that one of the strongest reasons I stay in the
fold is the lack of good alternatives, many of which I have tried.
Lord, to whom shall I go? The only thing more difficult than having
a relationship with an invisible God is having no such relationship.

REACHING FOR THE INVISIBLE GOD, 37–38

$\mathscr{W}$*hom have I in heaven but you? And earth has nothing
I desire besides you.*

PSALM 73:25

MARKED BY PASSION

*A*s I look back over the giants of faith, all had one thing in common: neither victory nor success, but *passion*. An emphasis on spiritual technique may lead us away from the passionate relationship that God values above all. The Bible emphasizes a relationship with a Person, and personal relationships are never steady-state.

From the spiritual giants of the Bible, I learn this crucial lesson about relating to an invisible God: Whatever you do, don't ignore God. Invite God into every aspect of life.

For some Christians, the times of Job-like crisis will represent the greatest danger. How can they cling to faith in a God who appears unconcerned and even hostile? Others, and I count myself among them, face a more subtle danger. An accumulation of distractions—a malfunctioning computer, bills to pay, an upcoming trip, a friend's wedding, the general busyness of life—gradually edges God away from the center of my life. Some days I meet people, eat, work, make decisions, all without giving God a single thought. And that void is far more serious than what Job experienced, for not once did Job stop thinking about God.

REACHING FOR THE INVISIBLE GOD, 188–89

*know your deeds, that you are neither cold nor hot. I wish you
were either one or the other! So, because you are lukewarm—
neither hot nor cold—I am about to spit you out of my mouth.*

REVELATION 3:15–17

ATROCIOUS MATHEMATICS

It was altogether in character for the scrupulous apostle Peter to pursue some mathematical formula of grace. "How many times shall I forgive my brother when he sins against me?" he asked Jesus. "Up to seven times?" Peter was erring on the side of magnanimity, for the rabbis in his day had suggested three as the maximum number of times one might be expected to forgive. "Not seven times, but seventy-seven times," replied Jesus in a flash.

The more I reflect on Jesus' parables, the more tempted I am to use the word "atrocious" to describe the mathematics of the gospel. I believe Jesus gave us these stories about grace in order to call us to step completely outside our tit-for-tat world of ungrace and enter into God's realm of infinite grace.

From nursery school onward we are taught how to succeed in the world of ungrace. Yet if I care to listen, I hear a loud whisper from the gospel that I did not get what I deserved. I deserved punishment and got forgiveness. I deserved wrath and got love. I deserved stern lectures and crawl-on-your-knees repentance; I got a banquet spread for me.

WHAT'S SO AMAZING ABOUT GRACE?, 63-64

Do not judge, and you will not be judged. Do not condemn, and you will not be condemned. Forgive, and you will be forgiven.

LUKE 6:37

A JUST GOD AFTER ALL

*A*mong many Christians an emphasis on future rewards has fallen out of fashion. In the United States, Christians have grown so comfortable that we no longer identify with the humble conditions Jesus addressed in the Beatitudes. Yet we dare not discount the value of future rewards.

I no longer scorn the eternal rewards mentioned in the Beatitudes as "pie in the sky." What good does it do to hope for future rewards? What good did it do the slaves to believe that God was not satisfied with a world that included back-breaking labor and masters armed with bullwhips and lynching ropes? To believe in future rewards is to believe that the long arm of the Lord bends toward justice, to believe that one day the proud will be overthrown and the humble raised up and the hungry filled with good things.

The prospect of future rewards in no way cancels out our need to fight for justice now, in this life. Rather, it allows us to believe in a just God after all. Like a bell tolling from another world, Jesus' promise of rewards proclaims that no matter how things appear, there is no future in evil, only in good.

THE JESUS I NEVER KNEW, 111–12

This is what the LORD Almighty says: "Administer true justice; show mercy and compassion to one another."

ZECHARIAH 7:9

FAITH UNDER FIRE

*P*aradoxically, difficult times may help nourish faith and strengthen bonds. I see this in human relationships, which tend to solidify in times of crisis. Seeing this principle lived out among people, I can better understand one of the mysteries of relating to God. Faith boils down to a question of trust in a given relationship. Do I have confidence in my loved ones—or in God? If I do stand on a bedrock of trust, the worst of circumstances will not destroy the relationship.

One Christian thinker, Søren Kierkegaard, spent a lifetime exploring the tests of faith that call into question God's trustworthiness. A strange man with a difficult personality, Kierkegaard lived with constant inner torment. Again and again he turned to biblical characters like Job and Abraham, who survived excruciating trials of faith. During their times of testing, it appeared to both Job and Abraham that God was contradicting himself. *God surely would not act in such a way—yet clearly God is.* Kierkegaard ultimately concluded that the purest faith emerges from just such an ordeal. Even though I do not understand, I will trust God regardless.

REACHING FOR THE INVISIBLE GOD, 53–55

But he knows the way that I take; when he has tested me,
I will come forth as gold.

JOB 23:10

TWO-HANDED FAITH

I am learning that mature faith, which encompasses both simple faith and fidelity, works the opposite of paranoia. It reassembles all the events of life around trust in a loving God. When good things happen, I accept them as gifts from God. When bad things happen, I do not take them as necessarily sent by God and I find in them no reason to divorce God. Rather, I trust that God can use even those bad things for my benefit.

A faithful person sees life from the perspective of trust, not fear. Bedrock faith allows me to believe that, despite the chaos of the present moment, God does reign; that regardless of how worthless I may feel, I truly matter to a God of love; that no pain lasts forever and no evil triumphs in the end.

God's style often baffles me: God moves at a slow pace, prefers rebels and prodigals, restrains power, and speaks in whispers and silence. Yet even in these qualities I see evidence of God's longsuffering, mercy, and desire to woo rather than compel. When in doubt, I focus on Jesus, the most unfiltered revelation of God's own self.

REACHING FOR THE INVISIBLE GOD, 65–67

For I am convinced that neither death nor life, neither angels nor demons, neither the present nor the future, nor any powers, neither height nor depth, nor anything else in all creation, will be able to separate us from the love of God that is in Christ Jesus our Lord.

ROMANS 8:38–39

SERENITY SOURCE

have visited Calcutta, India, a place of poverty, death, and irremediable human problems. There, the nuns trained by Mother Teresa serve the poorest, most miserable people on the planet. The world stands in awe at the Sisters' dedication and the results of their ministry, but something about these nuns impresses me even more: their serenity.

Their serenity traces back to what takes place before their day's work begins. At four o'clock in the morning, long before the sun, the Sisters rise, awakened by a bell and the call, "Let us bless the Lord." "Thanks be to God," they reply. Dressed in spotless white saris, they file into the chapel, where they sit on the floor, Indian-style, and pray and sing together. Before meeting their first "client," they immerse themselves in worship and in the love of God.

I sense no panic in the Sisters who run the Home for the Dying and Destitute in Calcutta. I see concern and compassion, yes, but no obsession over what did not get done. I pray that some day I will attain something like the holy simplicity these nuns embody.

REACHING FOR THE INVISIBLE GOD, 83–84

*And we, who with unveiled faces all reflect the Lord's glory,
are being transformed into his likeness with ever-increasing glory,
which comes from the Lord, who is the Spirit.*

2 CORINTHIANS 3:18

FAITH AT WORK

Some monastics describe an integrated life in which spiritual strength flows outward to bathe every activity. Then again, most of them live in spiritual communities. What about the rest of us, who face to-do lists that never get done and live in a culture that conspires to drown out silence and fill all pauses?

When I begin the morning by intentionally centering on God, from that still point I hope that serenity and peace will expand to affect the rest of my day. Yet I have found that even if I get *only* that half-hour of calmness in an otherwise jumbled day, the effort still proves worthwhile. I used to think that everything important in my life— marriage, work, close friends, relationship with God—needed to be in order. One defective area, like one malfunctioning program on my computer, would cause the entire system to crash. I have since learned to pursue God and lean heavily on God's grace even when, especially when, one of the other areas is plummeting toward disaster.

Exercising faith in the present means trusting God to work through the encounter before me despite the background clutter of the rest of my life. [My] very helplessness drives [me] to God.

REACHING FOR THE INVISIBLE GOD, 85–86

*Let us draw near to God with a sincere heart in full
assurance of faith, having our hearts sprinkled
to cleanse us from a guilty conscience.*

HEBREWS 10:22

THE GOOD LIFE

For a time I resisted thinking of God as an authority figure; harsh images from childhood had scarred too deep. Like many people, I saw religion mainly as a set of rules, a moral code handed down from an invisible world that we on this planet were somehow obligated to obey.

More recently, however, I have come to recognize that sometimes I submit gladly to authority. When my computer software acts up, I call technical support and scrupulously follow the technician's orders. And when I get hurt or sick, I see a doctor.

A doctor is probably the most helpful image for me to keep in mind while thinking about God and sin. Why should I seek out God's view on how to live my life? For the same reason I seek my doctor's opinion. I defer to my doctor, trusting that we share the same goal, my physical health, but that he brings to the process greater wisdom and expertise. And I am learning to view sins as spiritual dangers—much like carcinogens, bacteria, viruses, and injuries—that must be avoided. I am learning to trust that God wants the *best* life for me in this world, not some diminished, repressed life.

RUMORS OF ANOTHER WORLD, 128–29

You will keep in perfect peace him whose mind is steadfast,
because he trusts in you. Trust in the LORD forever,
for the LORD, the LORD, is the Rock eternal.

ISAIAH 26:3-4

JESUS AND PAIN

The fact that Jesus came to earth where he suffered and died does not remove pain from our lives. But it does show that God did not sit idly by and watch us suffer in isolation. God became one of us. All our questions about God and suffering should, in fact, be filtered through what we know about Jesus.

How did God-on-earth respond to pain? When he met a person in pain, he was deeply moved with compassion (from the Latin words *pati* and *cum*, "to suffer with"). Not once did he say, "Endure your hunger! Swallow your grief!" Very often, every time he was directly asked, he healed the pain.

The pattern of Jesus' response should convince us that God is not a God who enjoys seeing us suffer. I doubt that Jesus' disciples tormented themselves with questions like "Does God care?" They had visible evidence of God's concern every day: they simply looked at Jesus' face.

The record of Jesus' life on earth should forever answer the question, *How does God feel about our pain?* In reply, God did not give us words or theories on the problem of pain. God gave us himself.

WHERE IS GOD WHEN IT HURTS?, 225–26

He was despised and rejected by men, a man of sorrows,
and familiar with suffering.

ISAIAH 53:3

Tab. 36

MASTERY OF THE ORDINARY

Faith gets tested when a sense of God's presence fades or when the very ordinariness of life makes us question whether our responses even matter. We wonder, "What can one person do? What difference will my small effort make?"

Great victories are won when ordinary people execute their assigned tasks—and a faithful person does not debate each day whether he or she is in the mood to follow the sergeant's orders or show up at a boring job. We exercise faith by responding to the task that lies before us. I sometimes wish the Gospel writers had included details about Jesus' life before he turned to ministry. Did he ever question the value of the time he was spending as a carpenter on such repetitious tasks?

More often than I would care to admit, doubts gnaw away at me. I wonder about apparent conflicts in the Bible, about suffering and injustice, about the huge gap between the ideals and reality of the Christian life. At such times, I plod on, "acting as if" it is true, relying on the habit of belief, praying for the assurance that eventually comes yet never shields me against the doubts' return.

REACHING FOR THE INVISIBLE GOD, 90–91

By faith Abraham, when called to go to a place he would later receive as his inheritance, obeyed and went, even though he did not know where he was going.

HEBREWS 11:8

AN AUDIENCE OF ONE

*W*hen I worked as a young journalist for *Campus Life* magazine, my assistant kept a plaque on her desk with this two-line poem: "Only one life, 'twill soon be past. Only what's done for Christ will last."

Reading that plaque brought me up short every time. Although I believed its truth, how could I put it into practice? How *should* my faith in the invisible world affect day-to-day life in the visible world? According to Jesus, what other people think of me matters very little. What God thinks matters far more. I keep clamoring for attention and achievement. Jesus invites me to let go of that competitive struggle, to trust that God's opinion of me is the only one that counts, ultimately.

I ask myself how my life would differ if I truly played to an audience of One, if I continually asked not "What do I want to do?" or "What would bring me approval from others?" but "What would God have me do?" Certainly my sense of ego and rivalry would fade because I would no longer need to worry about proving myself to other people. I could concentrate instead on pleasing God, by living in such a way that would attract people to Jesus' style of life.

RUMORS OF ANOTHER WORLD, 68–69

Finally, brothers, we instructed you how to live in order to please God, as in fact you are living. Now we ask you and urge you in the Lord Jesus to do this more and more.

1 THESSALONIANS 4:1

WHAT GOD WANTS

For two weeks one winter I holed up in a mountain cabin in Colorado. I brought along a suitcase full of books and notes, but opened only one of the books: the Bible. I began at Genesis and when I finally made it to Revelation I had to call for a truck to unbury the driveway.

The combination of snow-muffled stillness, isolation from all people, and singular concentration changed forever the way I read the Bible. Above all else, this is what struck me in my daily reading: in theology books you will read of God's omnipotence, omniscience, and impassibility. Those concepts can be found in the Bible, but they are well buried and must be mined. Simply read the Bible and you will encounter not a misty vapor but an actual Person.

If you read the Bible straight through, as I did, you cannot help being overwhelmed by the joy and the anguish—in short, the passion— of the Lord of the Universe.

After two weeks of reading the entire Bible, I came away with the strong sense that God doesn't care so much about being analyzed. Mainly—like any parent, like any lover—God wants to be loved.

I WAS JUST WONDERING, 153–57

I will...praise your name for your love and your faithfulness,
for you have exalted above all things your name and your word.

PSALM 138:2

WHICH IS EASIER?

The Gospels tell of a paralytic who wanted so desperately to meet Jesus that he talked four friends into digging up a roof and lowering him through the hole! Apparently, Jesus rather enjoyed the interruption. Outstanding faith never failed to impress him. Yet his response baffled the observers. When Jesus saw *their* faith—plural, emphasizing the four friends' role in the healing—he said, "Take heart, son; your sins are forgiven."

Who said anything about sins? And who was Jesus to forgive them? Jesus hushed the debate with enigmatic words that seem to sum up his general attitude toward physical healing: "Which is easier, to say to the paralytic, 'Your sins are forgiven,' or to say, 'Get up, take your mat and walk'?"

How easily do we who live in material bodies devalue the world of spirit. It occurs to me that although Jesus spent much time on issues such as hypocrisy, legalism, and pride, I know of no television ministries devoted to healing those "spiritual" problems; yet I know of many that center on physical ailments. Just as I begin feeling smug, however, I remember how easily I feel tormented by the slightest bout with physical suffering, and how seldom I feel tormented by sin.

THE JESUS I NEVER KNEW, 173–75

"But that you may know that the Son of Man has authority on earth to forgive sins." He said to the paralytic, "I tell you, get up, take your mat and go home."

MARK 2:10–11

DOWNWARD SURRENDER

hoever tries to keep his life will lose it, and whoever loses his life will preserve it, Jesus said. Jesus' own life bears out that principle, for he experienced the loss as soon as he committed himself to public ministry. Crowds stalked him with ever-increasing demands. Opposition arose. Ultimately he lost his life.

Christians best influence the world by sacrificial love, the most effective way truly to change a world. Parents express love by staying up all night with sick children, working two jobs to pay school expenses, sacrificing their own desires for the sake of their children's. And every person who follows Jesus learns a similar pattern. God's kingdom gives itself away, in love, for that is precisely what God did for us.

Jesus did not disparage self-love: Love your neighbor *as yourself*, he commanded. Rather, he proposed that the highest fulfillment results from service to others, not narcissism. Some college students strike out for the wilderness or take up meditation in order to "discover themselves." Jesus suggests that we discover that self not by staring inward but by gazing outward, not through introspection but through acts of love. In the end, Jesus' prediction—"Whoever loses his life will preserve it"—proves true, for the downward surrender leads upward.

REACHING FOR THE INVISIBLE GOD, 244–46

*Greater love has no one than this, that he lay down
his life for his friends.*

JOHN 15:13

ORDINARY HEALERS

Not even God attempted a rationale for suffering in his reply to Job. The great king David, the righteous man Job, and finally even the Son of God reacted to pain much the same as we do. They recoiled from it, thought it horrible, did their best to alleviate it, and finally cried out to God in despair because of it. Personally, I find it discouraging that we can come up with no final, satisfying answer for people in pain.

And yet viewed in another way that nonanswer is surprisingly good news. When I have asked suffering people, "Who helped you?" not one person has mentioned a Ph.D. from Yale Divinity School or a famous philosopher. All of us have the same capacity to help, and that is good news.

No one can package or bottle "the appropriate response to suffering." Mainly, [people who are suffering] need love, for love instinctively detects what is needed. Jean Vanier, founder of L'Arche movement, says it well: "Wounded people who have been broken by suffering and sickness ask for only one thing: a heart that loves and commits itself to them, a heart full of hope for them."

WHERE IS GOD WHEN IT HURTS?, 168

If I have the gift of prophecy and can fathom all mysteries and all knowledge, and if I have a faith that can move mountains, but have not love, I am nothing.

1 CORINTHIANS 13:2

Profaning Money

esus saw money as something to guard against, not desire. "Where your treasure is, there your heart will be also," he said— an alarming thought to those of us who live in societies loaded with tangible treasure. He portrayed money as a negative spiritual force, a god named Mammon that pits itself against the kingdom of heaven. "You cannot serve both God and Money," he said bluntly.

[I used to think] I was using money to serve the kingdom of heaven. I came to see that I had missed the point of giving. I worried about exactly how much I should give, and to whom. I sought out the charities that offered the best return, the most result per dollar invested, and of course I expected a tax-deductible receipt and a thank-you note for my efforts. That kind of uptight, calculated giving is the opposite of what the Bible teaches. The apostle Paul mentions a hilarious, or cheerful, giver, and the hilarity comes because the act of giving is at its core irrational. It destroys the aura of worth surrounding money. By instinct we hoard money in steel vaults and secret caches; giving flagrantly sets it free, turning grace loose in a world of competition and balance sheets.

RUMORS OF ANOTHER WORLD, 210-11

Remember this: Whoever...sows generously will also reap generously. Each man should give what he has decided in his heart to give, not reluctantly or under compulsion, for God loves a cheerful giver.

2 CORINTHIANS 9:6–7

VAST SILENCE

We need look no further than the Bible for examples of God's absence.

"You have hidden your face from us," said Isaiah. "Why are you like a stranger in the land, like a traveler who stays only a night?" demanded Jeremiah. Any relationship involves times of closeness and times of distance, and in a relationship with God, no matter how intimate, the pendulum will swing from one side to the other.

I experienced the sense of abandonment just as I was making progress spiritually, advancing beyond childish faith to the point where I felt I could help others. Suddenly, the darkness descended. For an entire year, my prayers seemed to go nowhere; I had no confidence that God was listening.

When no "techniques" or spiritual disciplines seemed to work for me, in desperation I bought a book of hours used in high-church liturgy. Throughout that year I simply read the prayers and Bible passages, offering them to God as my prayers.

I now look back on that period of absence as an important growth time, for in some ways I had pursued God more earnestly than ever before. I came away with renewed faith and an appreciation of God's presence as gift rather than entitlement.

REACHING FOR THE INVISIBLE GOD, 242–43

How I long for the months gone by, for the days when God watched over me, when his lamp shone upon my head and by his light I walked through darkness!

JOB 29:2-3

No Fear

*N*early every time an angel appears in the Bible, the first words he says are "Don't be afraid!" Little wonder. When the supernatural makes contact with planet Earth, it usually leaves the human observers flat on their faces. But Luke tells of God making an appearance on earth in a form that does not frighten. In Jesus God finds at last a mode of approach that we need not fear. What could be less scary than a newborn baby?

According to the Bible, on earth Jesus is both God and man. But for Jews accustomed to images of God as a bright cloud or pillar of fire, Jesus also causes much confusion. How could a baby in Bethlehem, a carpenter's son, a man from Nazareth, be the Messiah from God? Jesus' skin gets in the way.

Why does God self-empty and take on human form? The Bible gives many reasons. The scene of Jesus as an adolescent lecturing rabbis in the temple gives one clue. For the first time, ordinary people can hold a conversation, a debate, with God in visible form. Jesus can talk to anyone—his parents, a rabbi, a poor widow—without first having to announce, "Don't be afraid!" In Jesus, God comes close.

MEET THE BIBLE, 405

Do not be afraid, for I am with you.

ISAIAH 43:5

TOO GOOD NOT TO BE TRUE

No summary of the prophets would be complete apart from one last message: their loud insistence that the world will not end in "universal final defeat," but in joy. Always, the prophets of the Old Testament got around to a word of hope.

Their voices soar like songbirds' when the prophets turn at last to describe the joy beyond the walls of the world. In that final day, God will roll up the earth like a carpet and weave it anew.

One day, says Malachi, we will leap like calves released from the stall. There will be no fear then, and no pain. Among the nations, peace will flow like a river, and armies will melt their weapons into farm tools. No one will complain about the hiddenness of God in that day. God's glory will fill the earth, and the sun will seem dim by contrast. For the prophets, human history is not an end in itself but a transition time, a parenthesis between Eden and the new heaven and new earth still to be formed by God. Even when everything seems out of control, God remains firmly in control.

DISAPPOINTMENT WITH GOD, 98–99

For you who revere my name, the sun of righteousness will rise with healing in its wings. And you will go out and leap like calves released from the stall.

MALACHI 4:2

GRACE DISPENSERS

*O*ne way in which Jesus' revolution affects me centers on how we are to view "different" people. Jesus' example convicts me today because I sense a subtle shift in the reverse direction. As society unravels and immorality increases, I hear calls from some Christians that we show less mercy and more morality.

Peter and Paul said we are to administer, or "dispense," God's grace. The image brings to mind one of the old-fashioned "atomizers" women used before the perfection of spray technology. Squeeze a rubber bulb, and droplets of perfume come shooting out of the fine holes at the other end. A few drops suffice for a whole body; a few pumps change the atmosphere in a room. That is how grace should work, I think. It does not convert the entire world or an entire society, but it does enrich the atmosphere.

I share a deep concern for our society. I am struck, though, by the alternative power of mercy as demonstrated by Jesus. Jesus never countenanced evil, but he did stand ready to forgive it. Somehow, he gained the reputation as a lover of sinners, a reputation that his followers are in danger of losing today.

WHAT'S SO AMAZING ABOUT GRACE?, 157–58

On hearing this, Jesus said to them, "It is not the healthy who need a doctor, but the sick. I have not come to call the righteous, but sinners."

MARK 2:17

THE GIFT NOBODY WANTS

*D*r. Paul Brand says with utter sincerity, "Thank God for pain!"
By definition, pain is unpleasant, enough so to force us to withdraw our
fingers from a stove. Yet that very quality saves us from destruction.
Unless the warning signal demands response, we might not heed it.

Pain is not God's great goof. The sensation of pain is a gift—the
gift that nobody wants. More than anything, pain should be viewed as a
communication network. A remarkable network of pain sensors stands
guard duty with the singular purpose of keeping me from injury.

I do not say that all pain is good. Sometimes it flares up and makes
life miserable. For someone with crippling arthritis or terminal cancer,
pain dominates so much that any relief, especially a painless world,
would seem like heaven itself. But for the majority of us, the pain
network performs daily protective service. It is effectively designed
for surviving life on this sometimes hostile planet.

Admittedly, the surprising idea of the "gift of pain" does not
answer many of the problems connected with suffering. But it is
a beginning point of a realistic perspective on pain and suffering.
Too often the emotional trauma of intense pain blinds us to its
inherent value.

WHERE IS GOD WHEN IT HURTS?, 33–35

We also rejoice in our sufferings, because we know that suffering produces perseverance; perseverance, character; and character, hope.

ROMANS 5:3–4

CAPTIVE AUDIENCE

*A*t each meeting on my 2006 tour of South Africa I told the story of Joanna, who embodies grace and reconciliation. When we went to Cape Town she invited us to Pollsmoor Prison, where she works. It's an amazing place, five separate prisons linked by underground tunnels, holding eight thousand prisoners in all, triple the expected number.

Several hundred men crowded into a kind of exercise room, and Joanna led the service. She has a remarkable presence, greets each prisoner by name, and commands respect from inmates and authorities alike. Most days the prisoners are allowed out of their cells for only one hour, so a chance to attend a church service is a welcome relief.

After the meeting we visited one of the three cells that the prison has designated as "Christian cells." There, we heard some of the prisoners' own stories. One by one they told of how God has changed their lives, and how they seek to live for God even if they never get out.

One scene stayed with me. Instead of pornography or graffiti, the prisoners had decorated their cell with the words of hymns and praise choruses. The most touching to me was "Surely the presence of the Lord is in this place."

TRIP NOTES, SOUTH AFRICA, 2006

But the Scripture declares that the whole world is a prisoner of sin, so that what was promised, being given through faith in Jesus Christ, might be given to those who believe.

GALATIANS 3:22

GRACE ABUSE

The potential for "grace abuse" was brought home to me forcefully. Late one night I sat in a restaurant and listened as my friend Daniel confided to me that he had decided to leave his wife of fifteen years. A Christian, Daniel knew well the personal and moral consequences of what he was about to do. His decision would inflict permanent damage on his wife and three children.

Then he dropped the bombshell: "Philip, you study the Bible. Do you think God can forgive something as awful as I am about to do?" Here is what I told my friend Daniel. "Can God forgive you? Of course. You know the Bible. God uses murderers and adulterers. For goodness' sake, a couple of scoundrels named Peter and Paul led the New Testament church. Forgiveness is *our* problem, not God's. What we have to go through to commit sin distances us from God— we change in the very act of rebellion—and there is no guarantee we will ever come back. You ask me about forgiveness now, but will you even want it later, especially if it involves repentance?"

WHAT'S SO AMAZING ABOUT GRACE?, 179–80

Today, if you hear his voice, do not harden your hearts.

HEBREWS 4:7

WHY BE GOOD?

*I*f I had to summarize the primary New Testament motivation for "being good" in one word, I would choose *gratitude*. Paul begins most of his letters with a summary of the riches we possess in Christ. If we comprehend what Christ has done for us, then surely out of gratitude we will strive to live "worthy" of such great love. We will strive for holiness not to make God love us but because God already does.

The best reason to be good is to want to be good. Internal change requires relationship. It requires love. "Who can be good, if not made so by loving?" asked Augustine. When Augustine made the famous statement, "If you but love God you may do as you incline," he was perfectly serious. A person who truly loves God will be inclined to please God which is why Jesus and Paul both summed up the entire law in the simple command, "Love God."

If we truly grasped the wonder of God's love for us, the devious question that prompted Romans 6 and 7—What can I get away with?—would never even occur to us. We would spend our days trying to fathom, not exploit, God's grace.

WHAT'S SO AMAZING ABOUT GRACE?, 190–91

We know and rely on the love God has for us. God is love.
Whoever lives in love lives in God, and God in him.

1 JOHN 4:16

PAIN'S MEGAPHONE

*W*e could—some people do—believe that the sole purpose of life is to be comfortable. But the presence of suffering vastly complicates that lifestyle—unless we choose to wear blinders.

It's hard to believe the world is here just so I can party, when a third of its people go to bed starving each night. If I try to escape toward hedonism, suffering and death lurk nearby, haunting me, reminding me of how hollow life would be if this world were all I'd ever know.

Suffering is a "rumor of transcendence" that the entire human condition is out of whack. Something is wrong with a life of war and violence and human tragedy. He who wants to be satisfied with this world, who wants to believe the only purpose of life is enjoyment, must go around with cotton in his ears, for the megaphone of pain is a loud one.

Of course, I can turn against God for allowing such misery. On the other hand, pain can drive me to God. I can believe God's promise that this world is not all there is, and take the chance that God is making a perfect place for those who follow God on pain-racked earth.

WHERE IS GOD WHEN IT HURTS?, 68–71

Do not let your hearts be troubled. Trust in God; trust also in me. In my Father's house are many rooms; if it were not so, I would have told you. I am going there to prepare a place for you.

JOHN 14:1-2

SEEKING THE GIVER

*O*n the surface, the book of Job centers on the problem of suffering. Underneath, a different issue is at stake: the doctrine of human freedom. Job had to endure undeserved suffering in order to demonstrate that God is ultimately interested in freely given love.

Satan's accusation that Job loved God only because "you have put a hedge around him," stands as an attack on God's character. It implies that God, alone, is not worthy of love; faithful people like Job follow God only because they are "bribed" to do so.

To understand this issue of human freedom, it may help to imagine a world in which everyone truly does get what he or she deserves. That world would be just and consistent, and everyone would clearly know what God expected. Fairness would reign. There is, however, one huge problem with such a tidy world: it's not at all what God wants to accomplish on earth. God wants us to choose to love freely, even when that choice involves pain, because we are committed to *God*, not to our own good feelings and rewards. God wants us to cleave, as Job did, even when we have every reason to deny God hotly.

WHERE IS GOD WHEN IT HURTS?, 89–91

Though he slay me, yet will I hope in him.

JOB 13:15

DISSONANT SYMPHONY

ost of us operate on a different scale of values than God. We would rank life as the greatest value. But clearly God operates from a different perspective. God indeed values human life, so much so as to declare it "sacred," meaning God alone has the right to take life. But in Noah's day, for example, God did not hesitate to exercise that right.

Similarly, many Bible passages show that some things are more awful to God than the pain of God's children. God did not even stay personally exempt from suffering. Do these show God's lack of compassion? Or do they, rather, demonstrate that some things are more important to God than a suffering-free life?

Is God speaking to us through our sufferings?. The message may simply be that we live in a world with fixed laws, like everyone else. But from the larger view, from the view of all history, yes, God speaks to us through suffering—or perhaps in spite of suffering. The symphony God is composing includes minor chords, dissonance, and tiresome fugal passages. But those of us who follow the conductor through early movements will, with renewed strength, someday burst into song.

WHERE IS GOD WHEN IT HURTS?, 94-95

Those who sow in tears will reap with songs of joy. He who goes out weeping, carrying seed to sow, will return with songs of joy, carrying sheaves with him.

PSALM 126:5-6

Tab. 36

WHITEWASHED

$\mathscr{A}$s I study the life of Jesus, one fact consistently surprises me: the
group that made Jesus angriest was the group that, externally at least,
he most resembled. What provoked such outbursts? They devoted their
lives to following God, gave away an exact tithe, obeyed every minute
law in the Torah, and sent out missionaries to gain new converts. Rarely
involved in sexual sin or violent crime, the Pharisees made model
citizens.

Overall, Jesus condemned the legalists' emphasis on externals.
"You Pharisees clean the outside of the cup and dish, but inside you
are full of greed and wickedness," he said. Expressions of love for
God had, over time, evolved into ways of impressing others.

Leo Tolstoy, who battled legalism all his life, understood the
weaknesses of a religion based on externals. According to Tolstoy,
all religious systems tend to promote external rules, or moralism.
In contrast, Jesus refused to define a set of rules that his followers could
then fulfill with a sense of satisfaction. The proof of spiritual maturity,
Tolstoy contended, is not how "pure" you are but awareness of your
impurity. That very awareness opens the door to grace.

WHAT'S SO AMAZING ABOUT GRACE?, 195–98

*Woe to you, teachers of the law and Pharisees, you hypocrites!
You give a tenth of your spices.... But you have neglected the more
important matters of the law—justice, mercy and faithfulness.*

MATTHEW 23:23

THE PARADOX OF PERSECUTION

In my visits to churches overseas, one difference from North American Christians stands out sharply: their view of hardship and suffering. We who live in unprecedented comfort seem obsessed with the problem of pain. Prayer meetings in the U.S. often focus on illnesses and requests for healing. Not so elsewhere.

I asked a man who visits unregistered house churches in China whether Christians there pray for a change in harsh government policies. After thinking for a moment, he replied that not once had he heard a Chinese Christian pray for relief. "They assume they'll face opposition," he said. "They can't imagine anything else."

I found the same pattern in Myanmar (formerly Burma). The person who invited me to the country informed me, "When you speak to pastors, you should remember that probably all of them have spent time in jail because of their faith." "Then should I talk about one of my book topics like *Where Is God When It Hurts?* or *Disappointment with God?*" I asked. "Oh, no, that's not really a concern here," he said. "We assume we'll be persecuted for faith. We want you to speak on grace. We need help getting along with each other."

*Among God's churches we boast about your perseverance and faith
in all the persecutions and trials you are enduring.*

2 THESSALONIANS 1:4

Tab. 36.

TRUE CONFESSION

salm 51, a poem of remembrance, may well be the most impressive outcome of David's sordid affair with Bathsheba. It is one thing for a king to confess a moral lapse in private to a prophet. It is quite another for him to compose a detailed account of that confession to be sung throughout the land!

All nations have heroes, but Israel may be alone in making epic literature about its greatest hero's failings. This eloquent psalm shows that Israel ultimately remembered David more for his devotion to God than for his political achievements. Step-by-step, the psalm takes the reader (or singer) through the stages of repentance.

In the midst of his prayer, David looks for possible good that might come out of his tragedy and sees a glimmer of light. He prays for God to use his experience as a moral lesson for others. Perhaps, by reading his story of sin, others might avoid the same pitfalls, or by reading his confession they might gain hope in forgiveness. David's prayer is fully answered and becomes his greatest legacy as king. The best king of Israel has fallen the farthest. But neither he, nor anyone, can fall beyond the reach of God's love and forgiveness.

MEET THE BIBLE, 216

Praise the Lord, O my soul, and forget not all his benefits—
who forgives all your sins and heals all your diseases,
who redeems your life...and crowns you with love and compassion.

PSALM 103:2-4

SOLOMON'S FOLLY

With everything imaginable working in his favor, at first it seemed
Solomon would gratefully follow God. Yet by the end of his reign
Solomon had squandered away nearly every advantage.

In one generation, Solomon took Israel from a fledgling kingdom
dependent on God for bare survival to a self-sufficient political power.
But along the way he lost sight of the original vision to which God
had called them. Ironically, by the time of Solomon's death, Israel
resembled the Egypt they had escaped: an imperial state held in place
by a bloated bureaucracy and slave labor, with an official state religion
under the ruler's command. Success in the kingdom of this world had
crowded out interest in the kingdom of God.

Solomon got whatever he wanted, especially when it came to
symbols of power and status. Gradually, he depended less on God and
more on the props around him. Success may have eliminated any crises
of disappointment with God, but it also seemed to eliminate Solomon's
desire for God at all. The more he enjoyed the world's good gifts, the
less he thought about the Giver.

DISAPPOINTMENT WITH GOD, 80–81

No one can serve two masters. Either he will hate the one and love the other, or he will be devoted to the one and despise the other.

MATTHEW 6:24

DO I MATTER?

I stand in the cashier line of the local supermarket and look around me. Does God know all these people by name? I ask myself. Do they really matter to him?

Sometimes when I watch the scenes of abortion protests and counter protests on the evening news, I try to envision the unborn who are prompting such ferocity. I have seen fetuses on display in museum jars to illustrate the progressive stages of human development. Worldwide, about six million of these tiny fetuses are disposed of each year—*murdered*, say the protestors. The image of God rests inside each one, say the theologians. What does God think of six million human beings who die never having seen the outside of a uterus? I wonder. Do they matter?

Novelist Reynolds Price said there is one sentence all humankind craves to hear: "The Maker of all things loves and wants me." That is the sentence Jesus proclaimed, loud as sweet thunder. The Maker of all things is the Maker of all human beings, an odd species that, unfathomably, is deemed worthy of individual attention and love. God demonstrated that love in person, on the gnarly hills of Palestine, and ultimately on a cross.

THE BIBLE JESUS READ, 201–6

See, I have engraved you on the palms of my hands.

ISAIAH 49:16

BEHIND THE CURTAIN

An encounter with the hiddenness of God may badly mislead.
It may tempt us to interpret God's hiddenness as a lack of concern.

The prophet Daniel had a mild encounter with the hiddenness of
God. Daniel puzzled over an everyday problem of unanswered prayer:
why was God ignoring his repeated requests? For twenty-one days
Daniel devoted himself to prayer. He called out to God, but received
no answer.

Then one day a supernatural being suddenly showed up on a
riverbank beside him. When he tried talking to the dazzling being,
he could hardly breathe. The visitor proceeded to explain the reason
for the long delay. He had been dispatched to answer Daniel's very
first prayer, but had run into strong resistance from "the prince of the
Persian kingdom." Finally, after a three-week standoff, reinforcements
arrived and Michael, one of the chief angels, helped him break through
the opposition.

Daniel's limited perspective distorted reality. The big picture
includes much activity that we never see. When we stubbornly cling
to God in a time of hardship, or when we simply pray, more may be
involved than we ever dream. It requires faith to believe that, and faith
to trust that we are never abandoned, no matter how distant God seems.

DISAPPOINTMENT WITH GOD, 235–37

*Now faith is being sure of what we hope for
and certain of what we do not see.*

HEBREWS 11:1

INSIDE INFORMATION

*A*part from the Old Testament we will always have an impoverished view of God. God is a Person who acts in history: the one who gave a promise to Noah, who called Abraham and introduced himself by name to Moses, who deigned to live in a wilderness *tent* in order to live close to his people. From Genesis 1 onward, God has wanted to be known, and the Old Testament is our most complete revelation of what God is like.

I admit that the Old Testament introduces some problems I would rather avoid. "Consider therefore the kindness and sternness of God," wrote Paul. I would rather consider only the kindness of God, but by doing so I would construct my own image of God instead of relying on God's self-revelation. I dare not speak for God without listening to God speak.

It makes an enormous difference how we picture God. Is God an aloof watchmaker who winds up the universe and steps back to watch it wind down on its own? Or is God a caring parent who holds not just the universe but individual men and women in his hands? I cannot conceive of a more important project than restoring a proper notion of what God is like.

THE BIBLE JESUS READ, 26–27

Taste and see that the LORD is good; blessed is the
man who takes refuge in him.

PSALM 34:8

PAIN TRANSFORMED

*P*aul makes a grand, sweeping statement in Romans, "And we know that in all things God works for the good of those who love him." That statement is sometimes twisted and made to imply that "only good things will happen to those who love God." As the rest of the chapter makes clear, Paul meant just the opposite.

Does God introduce suffering into our lives so that these good results will come about? Remember the pattern established at the end of Job. Questions about cause lie within God's domain; we cannot expect to understand those answers.

Instead, *response* is our assignment. The notion of suffering as productive brings a new dimension to our experience of pain. As we rely on God, and trust the Spirit to mold us in God's image, true hope takes shape within us. We can literally become better persons because of suffering. Pain can be transformed.

Where is God when it hurts? God is in *us*—not in the things that hurt—helping to transform bad into good. We can safely say that God can bring good out of evil; we cannot say that God brings about the evil in hopes of producing good.

WHERE IS GOD WHEN IT HURTS?, 108–9

*Those who suffer he delivers in their suffering;
he speaks to them in their affliction.*

JOB 36:15

Tab. 36

SMOOTHER THAN A BILLIARD BALL

*A*t first glance legalism seems hard, but actually freedom in Christ is the harder way. It is relatively easy not to murder, hard to reach out in love; easy to avoid a neighbor's bed, hard to keep a marriage alive; easy to pay taxes, hard to serve the poor. When living in freedom, I must remain open to the Spirit for guidance. I am more aware of what I have neglected than what I have achieved. I cannot hide behind a mask of behavior, like the hypocrites, nor can I hide behind facile comparisons with other Christians.

I once read that proportionally the surface of the earth is smoother than a billiard ball. The heights of Mount Everest and the troughs of the Pacific Ocean are very impressive to those of us who live on this planet. But from the view of Andromeda, or even Mars, those differences matter not at all. That is how I now see the petty behavioral differences between one Christian group and another. Compared to a holy and perfect God, the loftiest Everest of rules amounts to a molehill. You cannot earn God's acceptance by climbing; you must receive it as a gift.

WHAT'S SO AMAZING ABOUT GRACE?, 209–10

Trifolium pallidum.

Here there is no Greek or Jew, circumcised or uncircumcised, barbarian, Scythian, slave or free, but Christ is all, and is in all.

COLOSSIANS 3:11

JOLLY BEGGARS

*A*s a child, I put on my best behavior on Sunday mornings, dressing up for God and for the Christians around me. It never occurred to me that church was a place to be honest. Now, though, as I seek to look at the world through the lens of grace, I realize that imperfection is the prerequisite for grace.

My pride still tempts me to put on the best front, to clean up appearances. "It is easy to acknowledge," said C. S. Lewis, "but almost impossible to realize for long, that we are mirrors whose brightness, if we are bright, is wholly derived from the sun that shines upon us. Surely we must have a little—however little—native luminosity? Surely we can't be *quite* creatures. Grace substitutes a full, childlike and delighted acceptance of our need, a joy in total dependence. We become 'jolly beggars.'"

We creatures, we jolly beggars, give glory to God by our dependence. Our wounds and defects are the very fissures through which grace might pass. It is our human destiny on earth to be imperfect, incomplete, weak, and mortal, and only by accepting that destiny can we escape the force of gravity and receive grace. Only then can we grow close to God.

But he said to me, "My grace is sufficient for you, for my power is made perfect in weakness." Therefore I will boast all the more gladly about my weaknesses, so that Christ's power may rest on me.

2 CORINTHIANS 12:9

Tab. 36

CONTRACT FAITH

have observed that people involved in ministry, perhaps more so than most people, live with an unstated "contract faith." After all, they're giving time and energy to work for God; don't they deserve special treatment in return?

Bud, one of the true "saints" in urban ministry in Chicago, nearly cut off his hand on a power saw while demonstrating to volunteers how to build houses for the homeless. My friend Douglas has lived a Job-like existence in many ways, experiencing the failure of a ministry, his wife's death from cancer, and his own and a child's injuries by a drunk driver. Yet Douglas advises, "Don't confuse God with life."

When doubts arise, I often turn to that great chapter by Paul, Romans 8. "Who shall separate us from the love of Christ?" asks Paul. "Shall trouble or hardship or persecution or famine or nakedness or danger or sword?" In that one sentence, the apostle Paul summarizes his ministry autobiography. He endured all those trials for the sake of the gospel, and yet somehow he had the faith to believe that these "things"—surely not good in themselves—could nevertheless be used by God to accomplish good.

CHURCH: WHY BOTHER?, 92–94

The LORD *will fulfill his purpose for me; your love, O* LORD,
endures forever—do not abandon the works of your hands.

PSALM 138:8

SOUL THERAPY

The psalms give me a model of spiritual therapy. I once wrote a book titled *Disappointment with God*, and my publishers initially worried over the title, proposing instead *Overcoming Disappointment with God*. It seemed faintly heretical to introduce a book with a negative title into Christian bookstores filled with books on the marvelous Christian life. I found, however, that the Bible includes detailed accounts of people sorely disappointed with God—to put it mildly.

Not only Job and Moses have it out with God; so do Habakkuk, Jeremiah, and many of the unnamed psalmists. Some psalms merit titles like "Furious with God," "Betrayed by God," "Abandoned by God," "In Despair about God."

The odd mixture of psalms of cursing, psalms of praise, and psalms of confession no longer jars me as it once did. Instead, I am continually amazed by the spiritual wholeness of the Hebrew poets, who sought to include God in every area of life by bringing to God every emotion experienced in daily activity. One need not "dress up" or "put on a face" to meet God. There are no walled-off areas; God can be trusted with reality.

THE BIBLE JESUS READ, 120–23

Be merciful to me, O Lord, for I am in distress; my eyes grow weak with sorrow, my soul and my body with grief.

PSALM 31:9

CENTER STAGE

e all experience both an inner life and an outer life simultaneously. If I attend the same event as you, I will take home similar "outer"
facts about what happened and who was there but a wholly different
"inner" point of view. My memory will dwell on what impression I
made. Did I look good to others?

David seemed to view life differently. His exploits surely earned
him a starring role. Nonetheless, as he reflected on those events and
wrote poems about them, he found a way to make Jehovah, God of
Israel, the one on center stage. Whatever the phrase "practicing the
presence of God" means, David experienced it. He intentionally
involved God in the details of his life.

Throughout his life David truly believed that the spiritual world
was every bit as real as the "natural" world of swords and spears and
caves and thrones. His psalms form a record of a conscious effort to
reorient his own daily life to the reality of that supernatural world
beyond him. Now, centuries later, we can use those very same prayers
as steps of faith, a path to lead us from an obsession with ourselves to
the actual presence of our God.

THE BIBLE JESUS READ, 131

Surely you desire truth in the inner parts;
you teach me wisdom in the inmost place.

PSALM 51:6

ADVANCED SCHOOL

Somehow, David and the other poets managed to make God the gravitational center of their lives so that everything related to God. To them, worship was the central activity in life, not something to get over in order to resume other activity.

I am learning this daily process of reorientation, and Psalms has become for me a step in the process of recognizing God's true place at the gravitational center. I am trying to make the prayers first prayed by the Hebrew poets authentically my prayers.

I am sure that making the psalms my own prayers will require a lifelong commitment. I sense in them an urgency, a desire and hunger for God that makes my own look anemic by contrast. The psalmists panted for God with their tongues hanging out, as an exhausted deer pants for water. They lay awake at night dreaming of "the fair beauty of the Lord." They would rather spend one day in God's presence than a thousand years elsewhere. It was the advanced school of faith these poets were enrolled in, and often I feel more like a kindergartner. In reading the psalms, maybe some of it will rub off.

THE BIBLE JESUS READ, 132

*As the deer pants for streams of water,
so my soul pants for you, O God.*

PSALM 42:1

Tab. 36

DEMANDING ANSWERS

veryone has a built-in sense of justice. Frankly, much of the time life seems unfair. What child "deserves" to grow up in the slums? Why should people like Adolf Hitler get away with tyrannizing millions of people? Why are some kind, gentle people struck down in the prime of life while other, meaner people live into cantankerous old age?

We all ask different versions of such questions. And the prophet named Habakkuk asked them of God directly—and got a no-holds-barred reply. Habakkuk demands an explanation for why God isn't responding to the injustice, violence, and evil around him. [Habakkuk's] conversations with God convince him of one certainty: God has not lost control. A God of justice cannot let evil win.

"The earth will be filled with the knowledge of the glory of the Lord, as the waters cover the sea," God promises Habakkuk. A glimpse of that powerful glory changes the prophet's attitude from outrage to joy. In the course of his "debate" with God, Habakkuk learns new lessons about faith, which are beautifully expressed in the last chapter. God's answers so satisfy Habakkuk that his book, which begins with a complaint, ends with one of the most beautiful songs in the Bible.

MEET THE BIBLE, 322

Though the fig tree does not bud and there are no grapes on the vines, though the olive crop fails and the fields produce no food... yet I will rejoice in the LORD, I will be joyful in God my Savior.

HABAKKUK 3:17–18

FRANK CONFESSION

One issue comes up in virtually every one of Paul's letters: What good is the law? And whenever he starts talking about "the new covenant" or "freedom in Christ," the Jews want to know what he now thinks about that law.

Romans 7, the most personal and autobiographical chapter in Romans, discloses exactly what Paul thinks.

Paul never recommends throwing out the law entirely. He sees that it reveals a basic code of morality, an ideal of the kind of behavior that pleases God. The law is good for one thing: it exposes sin.

Romans 7 gives a striking illustration of the struggle that ensues when an imperfect person commits himself to a perfect God. Any Christian who wonders, *How can I ever get rid of my nagging sins?* will find comfort in Paul's frank confession. In the face of God's standards, every one of us feels helpless, and that is Paul's point precisely. No set of rules can break the terrible cycle of guilt and failure. We need outside help to "serve in the new way of the Spirit, and not in the old way of the written code." Paul celebrates that help in Romans 8.

MEET THE BIBLE, 594

*If Christ is in you, your body is dead because of sin,
yet your spirit is alive because of righteousness.*

ROMANS 8:10

JILTED LOVER

*M*any people carry around the image of God as an impersonal force. Hosea portrays almost the opposite: a God of passion and fury and tears and love. A God in mourning over Israel's rejection.

God uses Hosea's unhappy story to illustrate God's own whipsaw emotions. The powerful image of a jilted lover explains why, in a chapter like Hosea 11, God's emotions seem to vacillate so. God is preparing to obliterate Israel—wait, now God is weeping, holding out open arms—no, God is sternly pronouncing judgment again. Those shifting moods seem hopelessly irrational, except to anyone who has been jilted by a lover.

Hosea and God demonstrate in living color exactly what it is like to love someone desperately and get nothing in return. Not even God, with all power, can force a human being to love.

Virtually every chapter of Hosea talks about the "prostitution" or "adultery" of God's people. God the lover will not share the beloved bride with anyone else. Yet, amazingly, even when she turns her back, God sticks with her. God is willing to suffer, in hope that someday she will change. Hosea proves that God longs not to punish but to love.

MEET THE BIBLE, 282

*You must return to your God; maintain love and justice,
and wait for your God always.*

HOSEA 12:6

HANDLING DISAPPOINTMENT

I know too well my own instinctive response to the hiddenness of God: I retaliate by ignoring God. If God won't reveal himself to me, why should I acknowledge God?

The book of Job gives two other responses to such disappointment with God. The first was shown by Job's friends. Job's profound disappointment with God did not match their theology. Suppress your feelings, they told him. We know for a fact that God is not unjust. Shame on you for the outrageous things you're saying!

The second response, Job's, was a jarring counterpoint to his friends' relentless logic. "Why then did you bring me out of the womb?" he demanded of God. "I wish I had died before any eye ever saw me."

One bold message in the book of Job is that you can say anything to God. Throw at God your grief, your anger, your doubt, your bitterness, your betrayal, your disappointment—God can absorb them all. God can deal with every human response save one. God cannot abide the response I fall back on instinctively: an attempt to ignore God or act as though God does not exist.

DISAPPOINTMENT WITH GOD, 234–35

Listen to my prayer, O God, do not ignore my plea;
hear me and answer me.

PSALM 55:1-2

Tab. 30

UNFILTERED SUNLIGHT

I have often longed for God to act in a direct, closeup manner. But in the Israelites' dreary stories of failure I can perceive certain "disadvantages" to God acting so directly. Just as God found it nearly impossible to live among sinful people, the Israelites found it nearly impossible to live with a holy God in their midst.

Once, the great scientist Isaac Newton stared at the image of the sun reflected in a mirror. The brightness burned into his retina, and he suffered temporary blindness. Even after he hid for three days behind closed shutters, still the bright spot would not fade from his vision. If he had stared a few minutes longer, Newton might have permanently lost all vision. The chemical receptors that govern eyesight cannot withstand the full force of unfiltered sunlight.

There is a parable in Isaac Newton's experiment, and it helps illustrate what the Israelites ultimately learned from the wilderness wanderings. They had attempted to live with the Lord of the Universe visibly present in their midst; but, in the end, out of all the thousands who had so gladly fled Egypt, only two survived God's presence.

Is it possible that we should be grateful for God's hiddenness, rather than disappointed?

DISAPPOINTMENT WITH GOD, 73–75

The LORD *said to him, "Go down and warn the people so they do not force their way through to see the* LORD *and many of them perish."*

EXODUS 19:21

THE MAIN REASON

esus corrects my fuzzy conceptions of God. Left on my own, I would come up with a very different notion of God. My God would be static, unchanging. Because of Jesus, however, I must adjust those instinctive notions. (Perhaps that lay at the heart of his mission?) Jesus reveals a God who comes in search of us, a God who makes room for our freedom, a God who is vulnerable. Above all, Jesus reveals a God who is love.

Those raised in a Christian tradition may miss the shock of Jesus' message, but in truth love has never been a normal way of describing what happens between human beings and their God. Not once does the Koran apply the word *love* to God. Aristotle stated bluntly, "It would be eccentric for anyone to claim that he loved Zeus"—or that Zeus loved a human being, for that matter. In dazzling contrast the Christian Bible affirms, "God *is* love," and cites love as the main reason Jesus came to earth: "This is how God showed his love among us: He sent his one and only Son into the world that we might live through him."

"UNWRAPPING JESUS," *CHRISTIANITY TODAY*
JUNE 17, 1996

For God so loved the world that he gave his one and only Son,
that whoever believes in him shall not perish but have eternal life.

JOHN 3:16

SEEING UPSIDE DOWN

Taking God's assignment seriously means that I must learn to look at the world upside down, as Jesus did. Instead of seeking out people who stroke my ego, I find those whose egos need stroking; instead of the strong, I look for the weak; instead of the healthy, the sick. Is not this how God reconciles the world to himself? Did Jesus not insist that he came for the sinners and not the righteous, for the sick and not the healthy?

The founder of the L'Arche homes for the mentally disabled, Jean Vanier, says that people often look upon him as mad. He recruits skilled workers to serve and live among damaged people. Vanier shrugs off those who second-guess his choices by saying he would rather be crazy by following the foolishness of the gospel than the nonsense of the values of our world. Furthermore, Vanier insists that those who serve the deformed and damaged benefit as much as the ones whom they are helping. Even the most disabled individuals respond instinctively to love, and in so doing they awaken what is most important in a human being. Paradoxically, they replenish life in the very helpers who serve them.

RUMORS OF ANOTHER WORLD, 202–3

*God chose the foolish things of the world to shame the wise;
God chose the weak things of the world to shame the strong.*

1 CORINTHIANS 1:27

FUTURE REWARDS

One summer I met with a group of Wycliffe Bible Translators at their austere headquarters in the Arizona desert. I was impressed with the dedication of these professional linguists who were preparing for a life of poverty and hardship in remote outposts. They loved to sing one song especially: "So send I you, to labor unrewarded, to serve unpaid, unloved, unsought, unknown." The thought occurred to me that the song has it slightly wrong: these missionaries were not planning to labor unrewarded. They served God, trusting in turn that God would make it worth their while—if not here, then in eternity.

In the Beatitudes, Jesus honored people who may not enjoy many privileges in this life. To the poor, the mourners, the meek, the hungry, the persecuted, the poor in heart, he offered assurance that their service would not go unrecognized. They would receive ample reward. Wrote C. S. Lewis, "We are halfhearted creatures, fooling about with drink and sex and ambition when infinite joy is offered us, like an ignorant child who wants to go on making mud pies in a slum because he cannot imagine what is meant by the offer of a holiday at the sea."

THE JESUS I NEVER KNEW, 110–11

God is not unjust; he will not forget your work and the love you have shown him as you have helped his people and continue to help them.

HEBREWS 6:10

Tab. 36

GOD'S GAMBLE

I have learned that the church plays a vital, even necessary role. We are God's "new community" on earth. I am painfully aware that the ideal church is a mirage. Still, I must remind myself of Jesus' words to his disciples: "You did not choose me, but I chose you." The church was God's risk, God's "gamble," so to speak.

Several times I have read the Bible straight through, from Genesis to Revelation, and each time it strikes me that the church is a culmination, the realization of what God had in mind from the beginning. The body of Christ becomes an overarching new identity that breaks down barriers of race and nationality and gender and makes possible a community that exists nowhere else in the world.

My identity in Christ is more important than my identity as an American or as a Coloradan or as a white male or as a Protestant. Church is the place where I celebrate that new identity and work it out in the midst of people who have many differences but share this one thing in common. We are charged to live out a kind of alternative society before the eyes of the watching world.

CHURCH: WHY BOTHER?, 37–38

Let us not give up meeting together, as some are in the habit
of doing, but let us encourage one another—
and all the more as you see the Day approaching.

HEBREWS 10:25

DEFINING GRACE

God exists outside of time, the theologians tell us. God sees the future and the past in a kind of eternal present. If right about this property of God, the theologians have helped explain how God can possibly call "beloved" a person as inconstant, fickle, and temperamental as I am. When God looks upon my life graph, he sees not jagged swerves toward good and bad but rather a steady line of good: the goodness of God's Son captured in a moment of time and applied for all eternity.

Grace makes its appearance in so many forms that I have trouble defining it. I am ready, though, to attempt something like a definition of grace in relation to God. *Grace means there is nothing we can do to make God love us more*—no amount of spiritual calisthenics and renunciations, no amount of knowledge gained from seminaries and divinity schools, no amount of crusading on behalf of righteous causes. *And grace means there is nothing we can do to make God love us less*—no amount of racism or pride or pornography or adultery or even murder. Grace means that God already loves us as much as an infinite God can possibly love.

WHAT'S SO AMAZING ABOUT GRACE?, 69—70

So too, at the present time there is a remnant chosen by grace.
And if by grace, then it is no longer by works; if it were,
grace would no longer be grace.

ROMANS 11:5–6

Ellie Claire™ Gift and Paper Corp.
Minneapolis, MN 55438
www.ellieclaire.com

GRACE NOTES
Journal
© 2011 Philip Yancey

ISBN 978-1-60936-128-0

Cover Design: Gearbox

Printed in China.